SPIDERS SPIN WEBS

Written by Yvonne Winer

Illustrated by Karen Lloyd-Jones

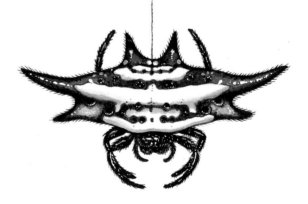

ini Charlesbridge

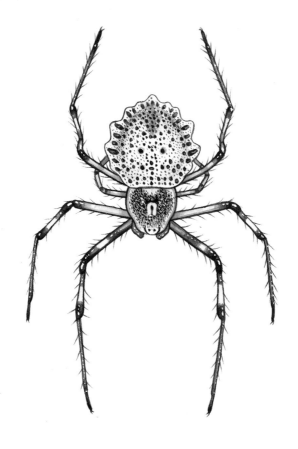

Spiders spin webs
Like weavers of old, as
Their spinneret patterns,
Like magic, unfold.
That's how spiders spin webs.

Spiders spin webs
On palettes of gold
Where their patchwork colors
Gaily unfold.
That's how spiders spin webs.

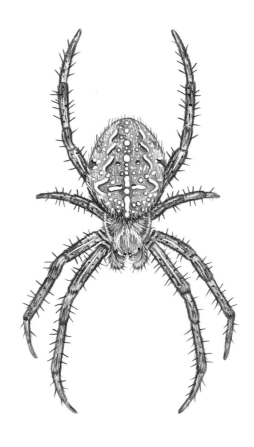

Spiders spin webs,
An incredible sight,
Like the sails of a galleon
In shimmering light.
That's how spiders spin webs.

Spiders spin webs
In mauve, green, and blue.
Upside-down rainbows
Painted in dew.
That's how spiders spin webs.

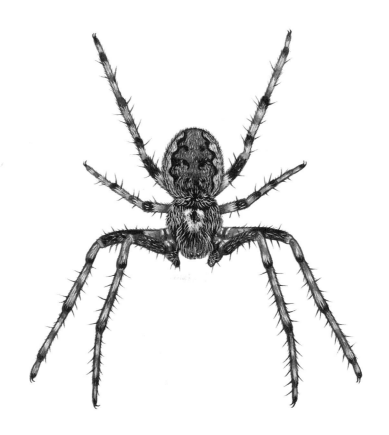

Spiders spin webs
When wintry winds blow,
Through summer and autumn
Or spring's gentle glow.
That's when spiders spin webs.

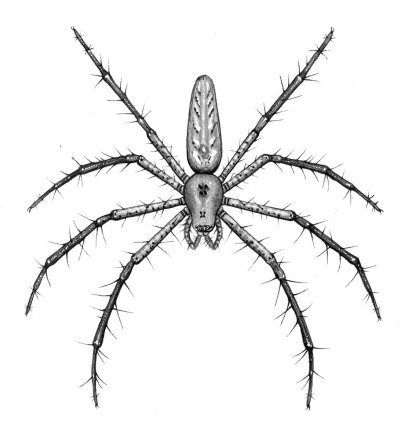

Spiders spin webs
In the heart of the night,
Weaving filigreed patterns
In the soft moonlight.
That's when spiders spin webs.

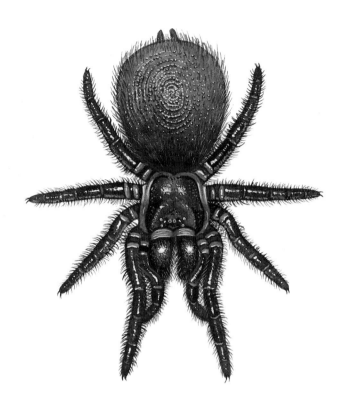

Spiders spin webs
In holes that are gloomy,
Holes that are stuffy,
And not very roomy.
That's where spiders spin webs.

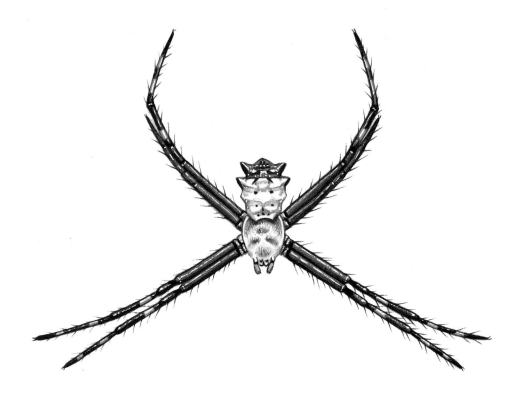

Spiders spin webs
Cradled in trees
That gently rock
In the cool autumn breeze.
That's where spiders spin webs.

Spiders spin webs
In impossible spaces,
Their shiny black eyes
Peer out at our faces.
That's where spiders spin webs.

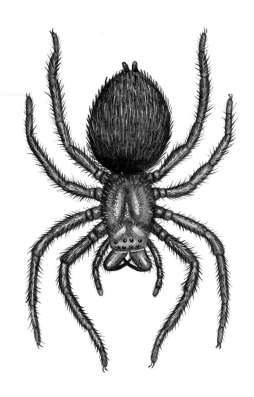

Spiders spin webs
Where still waters flow,
Trapping bubbles of air
Like crystals, below.
That's where spiders spin webs.

Spiders spin webs
A haven from heat,
A silken lined crevice,
A daytime retreat.
That's why spiders spin webs.

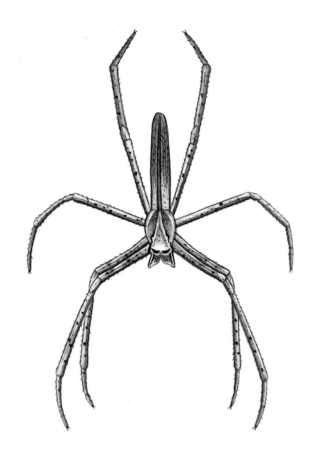

Spiders spin webs
That dance in the breeze
And trap tiny insects
In their flying trapeze.
That's why spiders spin webs.

Spiders spin webs
So gossamer light.
A lure of soft silk
For insects in flight.
That's why spiders spin webs.

Spiders spin webs
Their beauty unfolds.
A gift to the world.
A gift to our souls.
That's why spiders spin webs.

Spider Identification Guide

Spiders spin webs from silk secreted by spinning apparatus, called spinnerets, at the end of their abdomen. They either use their legs to draw the silk out of the spinnerets, or the wind will draw out the silk once the spider has attached itself to a surface. The silk itself is elastic and has a tensile strength greater than that of steel.

In addition to snaring prey, spiders use silk for a variety of purposes and some spiders can spin several different kinds of silk. Some use it to build secure homes away from their web; others use it to line burrows.

Females spin cocoons from silk, while males make use of silk to transfer sperm. Some small, young spiders drift on the wind over vast distances supported by a long thread of silk.

But it is in the traps to catch prey that we see the more familiar use of spider silk. The many different types of snares developed by spiders have made it possible for them to live in a wide range of ecosystems.

In this book, the word web is used in its broadest sense to include all purposes for which spiders use silk.

The spiders in this identification guide are arranged in the same order as the pages of this book. The small drawing in the left margin is a reduction of the drawing above each poem.

Kite spider
Gasteracantha falciformis   S. Africa
This spider builds a small circular web in low bushes. It remains in the web during the day, which is uncommon, but because its abdomen is hard and shiny and has several spiny projections, predators such as birds would probably find it inedible.

Most ornate herennia
Herennia ornatissima
East Asia and Australia
The small webs of these spiders are found stretched parallel to the surface of rock faces, tree trunks, or walls. Web repair and building are done in darkness, often in the early morning. Egg cocoons are white and covered in a papery layer of opaque silk. Males are much smaller than females and often live on the webs for up to thirty days. The web catches walking as well as flying insects.

American tarantula *Brachypelma vagans*   N. America
The reddish hairs on the spider's back are loosely attached and barbed. When attacked, the spider uses its back legs to comb out many barbed hairs that irritate the eyes and mouth of its pursuer, which soon gives up. The familiar characteristics of tarantulas—large size and hairy covering—do not apply to all members of this group. Many are small and some appear quite naked.

Garden orb web spider
Araneus diadematis   Europe
A common European spider that builds a sticky wheel-like web between shrubs and trees, this species can be found in open forests, heaths and domestic gardens. It produces a web 16 inches in diameter. Clusters of small spiderlings are common in early summer.

Garden spider
Eriophora transmarina   Australia
There are well over one hundred species in Australia, of which this is the most commonly known. This species is a heavily built and hairy spider. A variety of colors and designs is characteristic of the species, depending on an individual's immediate habitat. A gravid female can measure over an inch in body length, its large bulky abdomen 3/4 of an inch long. Their wheel-webs are often strung well above the ground.

Black orb weaver
Araneus sclopetarius   Gt. Britain
This member of the Araneidae family grows to a length of over half an inch and is often found near water, sometimes on bridges or on fences beside them.

Green lynx spider
Peucetia lucasii   Madagascar
Lynx spiders have unusually heavy spines on their legs. They share with the salticid spiders the ability to jump from surface to surface. The spider in the picture is seen guarding a substantial egg-sac typical of her genus. Characteristically large-eyed hunters, these spiders hunt actively upon vegetation, finding their prey visually and pouncing on it.

Trapdoor spider

Missulena bradleyi   Australia

Although this spider has a door on its burrow, it belongs to a different family from most other trapdoor spiders and is often referred to as a mouse spider. It constructs a burrow below ground, capped with a trapdoor. When the spider detects the vibrations of passing prey, it flips up the door, pulling its victim inside. The burrow is lined with silk to prevent wall collapse, as well as to provide a foothold.

Orb-weaving spider

Argiope argentata   America

The orb webs spun by these spiders have a prominent zig-zag pattern of silk in the center—the *stabilamentum*. It was thought that this prevented birds from flying into and damaging the web, but recent research has a more plausible answer. The silk in the stabilamentum reflects ultraviolet light, in the same way that flowers reflect ultraviolet light to attract pollinating insects. So it appears that the stabilamentum attracts insects to the web by mimicking a flower.

Wolf spider

Lycosa species   Worldwide

This spider is heavily dependent on its eyesight and earns its name by running its prey down with amazing speed. Four of its eight eyes are large and set in a square formation. The other four are smaller and in a row at the front. The burrow is usually lined with silk only at the entrance. However, a miniature silk wall, interwoven with grass and leaves, is sometimes constructed around the entrance. This helps prevent flooding by guiding water around, instead of into, the burrow.

Water spider

Argyroneta aquatica Europe & Asia

This spider spends its life beneath the surface of ponds and lakes. Only about half an inch in size, it builds a thimble-shaped underwater lair out of silk, attached to the stems of surrounding plants. Having done so, it swims to the surface and traps a bubble of air between its hind legs. It then swims down to its silken home and releases the bubble inside. Once the lair is complete and filled with air, the spider climbs inside, leaving only to catch prey or to replenish the air.

Mexican red-kneed tarantula

Brachypelma smithii   N. America

These spiders sometimes catch animals as large as small birds by lying in wait in holes in the ground. They are well adapted to their desert habitat, having a tough outer skeleton to cut down water loss, and they avoid the heat of the sun by being nocturnal. During the day they hide in rock crevices which they line with silk. Their popularity as pets has adversely affected natural populations.

Net-casting, web-throwing spider

Deinopis subrufa   Australia

This spider's web is unique to this family. Working only at night and using dry silk, it makes a simple, rectangular frame supported by horizontal threads. A ribbon of silk is then laid across it, zig-zag fashion. This is very cohesive and elastic, allowing the net to stretch to several times its relaxed dimensions. The spider then picks up four corners with its legs, and hangs upside-down, waiting for approaching prey. Net casters catch prey as large as crickets.

Crab spider

Misumena vatia   Europe

Slow-moving with a squat body, these spiders bear a striking resemblance to crabs, both in shape and habit of scuttling sideways. Their ability to change color to blend with their background provides them with excellent camouflage. They typically sit with their two powerful front pairs of legs held out ready to grasp any insect that comes too close. Their ability to kill insects several times their own size is testimony to the effectiveness of their venom.

Cave spider

Meta menardi   Europe

These small spiders are usually found near the opening of caves, where there is likely to be more prey. They feed mainly on flies and moths, but also prey on millipedes and cockroaches. In summer, each female spins a sac of silk and lays her eggs inside it. Then she seals the sac with more silk, to protect the eggs. These large egg sacs hang from the ceiling of the cave on long, thin threads. The following spring, young spiderlings hatch out of their eggs.

Author's dedication

For my granddaughter Bonnie Amelia and my great-nieces Cordelia, Francesca and Rowan.
May they inherit a wilderness.

Acknowledgments

Thanks to the following for their assistance with this book: Dr. Ron Atkinson, Senior Lecturer in the Faculty of Sciences,
University of Southern Queensland, Dr. Robert Raven, Museum Scientist (Spiders), Queensland Museum,
Dr. Michael Gray, Australian Museum, Sydney.

References and Recommended Reading

Amazing Spiders by Alexandra Parsons. New York, Random House, 1990.
Animal Artisans by Michael Allaby. New York, Random House, 1984.
The Book of Spiders and Scorpions by Rod Preston-Mafham. New York, Crescent Books, 1991.
British Spiders by G. H. Locket and A. F. Millidge. New York, Johnson, 1968.
Camouflage in Nature by Marco Ferrari. London, Prion, 1993.
* *Cave Life (Look Closer)* by Christiane Gunzi. New York, Dorling Kindersley, 1993.
* *Outside and Inside Spiders* by Sandra Markle. New York, Bradbury, 1994.
The Silken Web by Bert Simon-Brunet. Sydney, Reed, 1994.
Small Creatures of the Australian Wilderness by A. J. Press. Sydney, Weldon, 1984.
South African Spiders by Martin R. Filmer. London, Struik, 1992.
* *Spiders* by Norman Barrett. Danbury, CT, and New York, Franklin Watts, 1990.
Spiders by Lillian Bason. Washington, National Geographic Society, 1974.
Spiders by Lionel Bender. London, Gloucester, 1991.
* *Spiders* by Gail Gibbons. New York, Holiday House, 1993.
* *Spiders Near and Far* by Jennifer Owings Dewey. New York, Dutton, 1992.
The World of Spiders by W. S. Bristowe. London, Collins, 1958.
An asterisk (*) indicates titles recommended for children and widely available.

Internet Resources

The Arachnology Home Page: http://www.ufsia.ac.be/Arachnology/Arachnology.html
An index to all things relating to spiders and arachnology, the study of spiders, on the Internet.

Minibeast World of Insects and Spiders: http://www.tesser.com/minibeast/
Intended for insect and spider enthusiasts to "further the education and conservation of our minibeast world."

Spiders of Australia: http://www.xs4all.nl/~ednieuw/australian/Spidaus.html
An excellent personal site containing pictures of many Australian spiders.

An updated version of this list will be maintained at http://www.charlesbridge.com/spiders.html

First American Edition, 1998
Text copyright © 1996 by Yvonne Winer. Illustrations copyright © 1996 by Karen Lloyd-Jones
All rights reserved, including the right of reproduction in whole or in part in any form.

First published by Margaret Hamilton Books in 1996.
This edition published under license from Margaret Hamilton Books, a division of Scholastic Australia Pty. Limited.
Published by Charlesbridge Publishing, 85 Main Street, Watertown, MA 02472
(617) 926-0329 / www.charlesbridge.com

Library of Congress Cataloging-in-Publication Data is available.

ISBN 0-88106-983-3 (reinforced for library use). ISBN 0-88106-984-1 (softcover)

Printed in Hong Kong
(hc) 10 9 8 7 6 5 4 3 2
(sc) 10 9 8 7 6 5 4 3 2

The illustrations in this book were done in watercolour, gouache, and airbrush.
Typeset in 18 pt. Bernhard by Silver Hammer Graphics.